A Sailor's Wife,

Volume One

Written by: B.L. Fleischer

Emery Press, LLC
Fort Lauderdale, FL
www.emerypressbooks.com

All rights reserved

First Edition – December 2018

Copyright 2018 – Bethany Fleischer

No part of this book may be reproduced or transmitted in any form or by any means, electronic or mechanical, including photocopying, recording, or by any information storage and retrieval system, except as permitted by law. For additional information contact Emery Press, LLC.

ISBN (Trade): 978-0-9600505-0-5
ISBN (eBook): 978-0-9600505-1-2

Cover Design by Aaron Smith
Editing by Grammar Goddess Editing

Dedicated to my sweet mother, who was also a sailor's wife, and who left this earth on December 9th, 2017.

This volume of A Sailor's Wife *is a collage of true stories, desires, and personal intimate moments that all women crave.*

Chapter One: A Lover's Quarrel

Quarrel is defined by Webster as, "a ground of dispute or complaint."

AS A CONFIDENT, gorgeous, and broken young female who knew absolutely nothing about life, I had a feeling of loss in this world that has so much to offer. I determined at a very young age that I was not going to fall into the same problems like so many before me had self-inflicted upon themselves. I have seen relationships implode before the first kiss. I was watching for clues and patterns of behavior that triggered a fight or an outcome that I did not want for myself.

I am a third-generation sailor's wife; my mother was married to a sailor, and her mother before her. Heaven is where we treasure them now. The ebb and flow of this lifestyle is tough.

My grandmother was raised in a Catholic orphanage; her parents could not afford to take care of her and her two sisters.

In the 1930s families were not large. The average family size was four, with an annual income of about one thousand dollars.

On a blind double date, she met her mate. My grandfather was a traditional man who worked hard to provide for his family, but was away most of the time. He was a submarine sailor and the only communication he had with his family while deployed was via familygram.

Familygrams were letters that sailors and their families exchanged once a month and were censored by the military. Which meant, if something was written with a negative tone or comment in the message, it would be deleted from your personal message intended for your spouse. If the washer was broken or you were depressed, you could not share it with your other half.

My grandmother was not happy with this lifestyle. She survived with her music and a drink, but she was lonely.

My mother, being her first born of five children, became a natural nurturer, filling in when my grandfather was away.

One rainy night, my grandfather tried to surprise his family after a long deployment. It had been such a long time that the family dog didn't recognize this bearded, soaked man who walked in. The dog was so frightened that he took a dump right in front of him. That is a fantastic homecoming for anyone.

My mother's relationship with her parents was strained. She had taken on a role that wasn't hers to take on, but her instincts could not have been truer. My parents met in high school and became high school sweethearts. My sweet mother tutored my father in Math and dad introduced mom to religion. As they grew closer, my mother offered to take her sisters and brothers to church.

My grandmother did attend one revival night service and was treated unkindly.

She was new and not familiar with the church's customs. She wore slacks and lipstick, while the other ladies were covered from ankle to wrist, wearing skirts or dresses, and fresh-faced. The church started singing a verse of a song that was not the original lyrics. "There is a painted lady in the church! There is a painted lady in the church!" This hurt my grandmother and she never took up religion again.

As soon as my mother could leave her childhood home, she did. My mother had her first child around the time my grandmother had her last. My uncle and my only brother are a few months apart.

I am from a semi-large family with unlimited dysfunction. I've witnessed things that no young person should ever have to witness. One occasion, when I was little, while my mother was working midnight shifts trying to make ends meet, my sailor father cut off the tip of his finger chopping wood.

As a young girl that was terrifying, but we handled it by drawing strength from within and dealing with the situation at hand.

Normal seemed nowhere in sight, but I wasn't looking for normal. I never wanted to follow the current trends or style. Honestly, I had no financial say in the matter, due to our one-income household.

As a sailor's wife, you learn, and you learn fast. Some wives don't last, and others are the perfect mate. Then there are the ones like me. The type of person who does whatever it takes to make love happen wherever we are. You see, there's a ton of trust, support, and sacrifice that a sailor and his wife must be willing to endure. It can be as blissful as your perfect wedding day or as bad as your child throwing up on himself in the car because he's crying so hard because his daddy just said goodbye before a deployment.

Moments like these are the ones my mother experienced four times over. Four sailor children; that's a lot to keep up with. I barely survived living it with one sailor child.

I want to pull my mother's strength through these stories and messages. My vision for this book is to honor her and share our moments as women, mothers, daughters, friends, family, and as a sailor's wife. Secrets we hold as divine creators that should be shared. We could use more kindness and divvying up secrets that help each other in our world today.

Homecomings are always amazing, though, and every new place we've lived has been a refreshing change, at least at first. It realistically takes some time to know whether or not you truly like a new location. One must feel the new vibe that the area gives you. During these transition times is when you learn about yourself. Is it welcoming or stiff? Is it a place we can adapt to?

Many wives do extensive research on the new area once we know where we may be heading. My parents didn't have that luxury or the technology in the '70s. As children, we moved with my father a few times. Mom never had a say nor complained.

This first period of my life was spent in the south, growing up alongside other sailor families. It seemed that my father was deployed for years at a time. My memories of those times seem distorted and faded. Glimmers of another life. Others I recall quite clearly, like when I almost died at the age of five from an illness, biting my tongue off when I was a teething infant, or sleep walking and talking.

Born the middle girl, I recall when I was the first of my sisters to experience something, such as getting my period or having sex. This created a sense of comparison for my Irish twins. I also recall my focused mom working her tail off until she just couldn't do it anymore for her family. All the time!

Being a parent now and having the privilege to be married to my hero, a man who loves me wholeheartedly, a person who never seems to do anything wrong, is a dream I have never dreamt. He's not perfect, but he is made perfectly for me. The ying to my yang.

I wish my goddess mother could have had that. She wanted it and tried with my father, but some just cannot reciprocate these feelings. Moving can be aging and feels like a mixed bag of pressure pointed massages. A constant lover's quarrel, knowing you are supporting an all-American hero, all the while trying to make strides on your own dreams.

A sailor's wife has desires, goals, and dreams just like any other person. I've always had big dreams, and thankfully, have been able to keep my goals moving in the right direction; forward! My mother, on the other hand, became accustomed to my father's behavior. She wanted to be a nurse and was a caretaker by nature.

My mother was so caring and supportive. Always there for her children in any capacity she could. Her children were first in her life, but my father was just as high maintenance as all five of us put together. She died the way she lived, by the second! One breath at a time, one moment at a time.

She never had the wealth of secure grandioso accounts, rather her wealth lied within. The nurturer everyone needed. The evolution of one's life should be shared, and it should be treasured. As I share my experiences through my reflections of my mother, I have my fingers crossed in hopes that she experienced similar treasured moments in her own ways that are unbeknownst to me.

Since being a sailor's wife, we have lived in five different cities: Tampa and Miami, Florida; Pascagoula, Mississippi; Havelock, North Carolina; and Nantasket Beach, Massachusetts. These places are all so vastly different culturally and socially.

The pressure is real. The pressure that not only military wives, but all mothers put on themselves is unbelievable. Trying to be the perfect wife, a Proverbs mother, the person she is on the inside, and not losing herself while stabilizing a household.

We teach our children and our loved ones to be true to themselves while giving away a piece of ourselves in return.

I learned the hard way that even if you do the right thing and treat people the way you want to be treated that they do not always return what is known as "The Golden Rule."

It is a true benefit of being married to a sailor to have the luxury of experiencing different places and cultures. And the lover's quarrel rears its ugly head when you are forced to say goodbye to the friends who have become family, good jobs, and amazing neighbors. The kind of neighbors who would cook for you without a second thought, just because they knew you were home alone and needed a hand.

Those are the neighbors you never knew you needed or even dreamed of having. That is where the lover's quarrel feels like your heart will burst. Your heart hurts with the truth of losing another friend because your best friend, lover, hero must move on.

Passion is what one calls a career path that doesn't require the feeling of dread to do it day after day. My sweet mother was fiercely passionate.

She created four unique offspring; we probably keep her busy still today. After one passes away, no matter the relation to the person, it changes us. In some way, in some light things, look different. When you lose the matriarch of your family, your center, the person who brings all the uncomfortable together, everything changes. Mom was with us, caring for her grands, before she died in New England.

Chapter Two: A Lover's Passion

Passion is defined by Webster as, "a strong liking, desire for or devotion to some activity, object, or concept; the emotions as distinguished from reason."

HAVE YOU EVER recalled a passionate moment and felt the residual spark from that moment? You get the feeling like your soul is vibrating? That's passion. I call those vibrations the "aftershocks" of life's purest moments. My passion has wants and needs. A sailor's wife desires this passionate feeling from her mate. I want to see fire in my sailor's eyes when he glances my way. That desire also takes effort. It's not just an "I love you" as you pass in the hall or a kiss that doesn't connect with a moment.

Those moments are what I call experiencing the "friend zone" of a relationship. This "friend zone" is real and is like a lack of connection with your partner. It can even feel like a space or distance amongst the two of you, even as you embrace.

These moments are normal, but can be tough to get through.

Every bond takes work; whether it be with friends, family, or your spouse. Everything you want attention from needs your attention in return to keep the relationship thriving. Many close women friends have shared with me similar feelings of passion and desire. But like so many before me, those feelings weren't as important as they are now. So, why now?

After tragically losing my mother, I was left with an empty hole in my chest feeling that I'm still grappling with as I share these encounters. Some say that this is grief and that time will heal the painful emptiness. Others say that this feeling can be described as, "all the love I want to give my mother but cannot." The reason I bring up this experience with my loss to light is because at that moment my sailor was taking care his family and mine. My mother passed away in our home and it shattered our whole world.

This collection of her experiences mixed with my lack of my experience is devoted to her.

As of the publication of this volume, my mother has been gone one year. And one year later, I'm just starting to feel again.

That's why. Writing has become a form of healing. My mother loved to write. I never thought in a million years that I would be writing a book; ever.

I was trying to find a way to honor her for her one-year anniversary. I kicked around the thought of raising money and donating it to the facility that she died in or donating money to a cause she believed in.

One night in September, I was talking to my husband and decided she had so much to share, lessons I have learned from her, and this book could let her live forever. I started writing that evening and set this new adventure into motion.

It felt right. It felt good.

The death of my mother made everything feel different, experiences and emotions are magnified, and my senses are electric. I went numb when it happened and to start to feel again is a welcomed sensation. Yes, I know I'm grieving and not one person grieves the same, but it's a world-changing event in my life.

She's been a part of my everyday life. Now, she continues to shine through us, her family. On the ninth of every month, I feel my soul shutting down. I try to be quiet and stay in these days, thinking, *It would be nice to talk to mom...* Light a candle.

Thinking, *Miss you dearly, mom!*

As I write, I am so grateful to have a mate who is the best thing to ever happen to me. His unfailing love and astounding commitment to me is beyond words. I wish this type of relationship for everyone, and most of all, I wish and hope my mother felt this at some point during her life. To be able to freely explore the realms of your own passion with a person who believes in you all the time with no doubts.

My husband embraced my family and supported them as he did me. An unbelievable sacrifice many cultures do timelessly. He is my passion, priority, and my prince. I try to keep those thoughts in the forefront of my mind, because he also tends to drive me nuts. Marriage is hard. Commitment is hard.

It takes that "tough love" mentality to a whole new level. I never want to forsake him, and we choose to be loyal to our marriage vows. I never want to sound like my mother or his mother, for that matter. I do not baby him, but I do adore him. We have agreed, God forbid, if anything were to happen to either of us, we would never get married again. One and done! It's work!

My parents lived by that motto, it seems. My father's military career seems to have come first – before his family – and that is something we chose to accept. This can be hard though when the kids are sick, or it's a special occasion, like the holidays and birthdays.

My gracious mother would put on a display every holiday for us kiddos. The holidays, with four young children, were like a fairy tale. Tons of gifts, and if you didn't like your gift, you had three others to trade with. Holidays were a happy time. Mother died two weeks before Christmas of 2017. That December felt nonexistent! It felt like time stopped.

This year I am releasing this book, *A Sailor's Wife, Volume One* in honor of you, mom. You will forever live on through this book.

A mother's passion also must be acknowledged. As a mother, one wants to be the best she can be, so our protégés can have better livelihoods than the one before them.

This is ridiculous. What are we teaching ourselves as women? We are enough and shouldn't feel like we must make anything better for anyone, but we do. Paying it forward is a great act of kindness and saying, but not when it becomes enabling or expected.

My mister isn't always around, but we make it work. Passion is what it takes to make it as a sailor's wife. This can be a missing element in our men's lives. Most men are not wired or made this way; my sailor is definitely not. However, as the mom and wife, I help share that load for the both of us. That is the type of partnership that we have as friends, adults, and lovers.

My mother missed this connection with my father. This component in a relationship isn't a wish, it's a necessity. Some men must be taught, a few get it, and others are just lazy lumps. You must share the load and make your desires and needs known.

You may notice that I refer to lovers in several different contexts; I have always loved the word. "Lover" can be used to refer to a person. It can also be used as an action. I believed for a very long time that love would heal all things. I have recently discovered that love is not always enough. This thought, this revelation saddened me.

Doing the right thing isn't always enough!

Treating others the way you would like to be treated is not always enough! So, what is enough?

Chapter Three: A Lover's Part

Part is defined by Webster as, "one of the often indefinite or unequal subdivisions into which something is or is regarded as divided and which together constitute the whole."

AS COMPLEX AS we all are, there is a part of us that wants to be adored. This adoration includes chivalric romance, intimacy that makes you feel like you are melting inside, and the feeling of being secure. Safe to explore our needs. This love… this love is addicting! When you are in a safe place, with the right person at the most perfect time, magic happens. This is the lover's part that a sailor's wife must create when home. It is equally important that your mate creates this magic for you in return.

I remember when our child was conceived on Valentine's Day. Dearest husband to be took me to our favorite pub and then home for an after party.

I walked into a dim room with a rose petal covered bed and lit candles.

Part of me believes that these types of efforts will help keep my marriage strong and fresh. I understand that most of the time marriage isn't magical, but if *you* don't make it magical, then who will? One must give to receive. Parenting and marriage are work! I do not recommend it for the faint-hearted. Here in our homeland, fewer and fewer couples stay married. Couples marry sometimes only for hours. This is such a shame. These marriages make the word "marriage" mean less. My part in being married to a sailor is being the person who thinks of everything that he forgets.

We truly work hard at it and try have fun at the same time. I try to make each moment count, which can be truly exhausting. I don't want to have any regrets but, as I age, you bet I do. Wishing constantly that my mother knew I learned this trait from her. Hoping she knows that we recognize her in our hearts and lives, daily.

I like the part in my marriage when I get to do all the things to him that no other person is allowed to. Fantasies, dreams, trips, fights, and making-up… whatever it takes. For better or worse. This sailor's wife is also a planner. My mind never seems to quiet. This restlessness is a new part of my norm.

As trials arise and life gets hectic, I recommend doing something nice for yourself. Buy your favorite dessert or get a pedicure. Quiet time becomes a peaceful welcome to your routine. Listen to yourself, be kind to yourself. Self-talk becomes the only talk, sometimes. Love yourself so others will see that love. Obviously, I choose to take a positive disposition, but there are times that my own voice annoys me. Military wives are known to be the support behind our forces. Many times, we are left behind to undertake who knows what and a little bit of everything else on the side.

There are times of total madness and other times of uncontrollable joy. That seems to be how life goes.

I think back at my childhood and relish thoughts of my lovely mother doing all of this with her sailor's four children. How did she manage? With the constant ebb and flow of the energy in our universe. There will always be ups and downs but today it feels more like, "we are hanging in and holding on tight!" with life.

My part, as the mother of my sailor's son, is super tricky. I must play both the good and bad parent when necessary. Single mothers, hands down, are my heroes. To juggle everything and still smile when you want to just collapse and drown in a box of something. These women are the *real* "wonder women."

Then I think of my loving mother and realize the magnitude of worries and wonder she had for us. We both had "part-time" husbands.

A part-time husband is a combination of being married sometimes and being a single parent most of the other time. Some would say this is the best of both worlds. Parenting being one of the toughest jobs known to man, is a major part of being a sailor's wife.

Sometimes you have to parent other sailors' babies. Sailor wives normally stick together, dine together, and generally help each other out. As we're informed of our spouse's mission we could share the details amongst ourselves, but what we knew was only what our husbands could tell us. Military families become part of your extended family and are a close-knit unit.

Growing up, we had an array of military family friends. Some we still speak to today. We knew together, collectively, that they were all experiencing the same issues. We thought this was the way it was everywhere, and my mom certainly did her part.

The wives and military families I've met seem fair-weathered. Some wives acted like they were the actual person serving. In truth, military wives are just normal people who support their spouses who serve our great country. Some women try to act like they oversee you; others just follow along. As an alpha female, neither worked for me.

Once, we were living on a Marine Corps base and I had a meeting with the base moms about volunteering at our local school. At that time, my dear husband was a lower rank than many of these women's spouses. They treated me respectfully but in a rude, entitled manner. It seemed they thought they were higher ranking than me. It's not ok for someone to act like they're wearing their spouse's rank. They were just like me, and I let them know it. Fearlessly, I was doing my part. I was not at the meeting to be belittled nor did I let it happen. They all ended up volunteering and I was honored with a county award.

Chapter Four: A Lover's Fury

Fury is defined by Webster as an, "intense, disordered, and often destructive rage; one who resembles an avenging spirit; *especially*: a spiteful woman."

I LEARNED TO field questions that need my personal opinion with this reply, "Which answer do you want me to tell you? The truth or what you want to hear?"

I feel like this is a safe reply and an honest response to the question. I'm known for my honesty. I believe that our thoughts are all-important. We should feel free to speak our mind. I'm never cruel or purposefully trying to hurt someone, but don't ask me a question unless you want MY answer. I get myself into so much trouble this way.

I've been told, "You don't believe in telling lies at all, and you will suffer the consequences of that periodically because sometimes people just don't want to hear the truth. While admirable, you're unlikely to have a lot of people who want to listen."

When I asked my friend a simple question, "How are you?" I had to stop and take a mental note of his response.

He retorted, "Which answer do you want me to tell you? The truth or what you want to hear?"

I had thought it was an easy question. That's what I get for thinking. This guy is such a fun, good-hearted person. He knows I'm married to a sailor and has become part of our New England family. Nonetheless, the fury I saw in his gorgeous baby blue eyes was intense. Fury is real. His fury shows in the way he walks, talks, and breathes toward his lover whom he ferociously loves.

I remember the day I met him. We were new to town and stepped into this pub for the first time. My hairclip fell on the floor and this blue-eyed hunk picked it up. He handed it back to me and I told him it wasn't mine, but was my bald sailor's. We all laughed. We chatted for a few moments and introduced ourselves to him and the barkeep.

I saw a spark in him, not towards me, but toward the barkeeper.

I looked at him and said, "How long have you loved her?"

He replied in the softest, most passionate manner, "Forever."

My heart melted.

Some people have these kindred connections; instant feelings. We attract the people who we are most like. A lover's fury is sensual and hot. Lover is used as a verb in this passage. Sailor wives want to stay on point with what their spouses desire. My sailor chooses to remain loyal and faithful to our commitment to each other. He has had the chance to sow his seed elsewhere, many times. He's worked in many states and countries. Fury and trust go hand in hand in any long distant relationship. After he returns home from a trip, I know my loins are screaming and it's pretty obvious his are, too. That's a lover's fury, the need to be touched, kissed, and adored.

A SAILOR'S WIFE

My parents survived a 50-plus-year marriage. That was a different type of fury.

In the '70s, the military didn't have the communication technology of today's military. My mother would wait for word from her sailor for weeks, sometimes months. Sometimes it would be a letter delivered by snail mail, other times it would be a VHS tape (that's a recording of him, for you younglings). Thankfully, today we have social media for quick daily, "hello and how are you doing?" communications. Social media can be super wicked, though.

I like to reconnect with loved ones. I also like to unplug from all electronics and spend quality time with the people I adore. Time is the one irreplaceable thing you can give. It's also the most valuable thing you can give to someone. Some say time is money. My mom wanted the time we had together to count. She was fun and good at keeping us busy while my dad was away. When her sailor returned home, though, things changed.

My sailor father was hot-blooded and didn't seem like the logical father figure. He was born a coal miners' son. When he was little more than a baby, his father was murdered in his presence. Such an early-age trauma can haunt you for life. His mother became a minister and remarried. My father was quickly joined by four sisters. They adored my dad and called him, Bubba. He became a sailor in the '70s. My mother spent most of her time trying to balance my father with her efforts to keep a happy home while he was present. It so happens that some have a natural parenting instinct and others not so much. Unfortunate for his children. I'm proud to be one of their children. My father had more of the angry fury, and he could be cruel. Mom could be equally as furious and cruel, but in a protective way for her children.

How they made it to the end married, one may never know? Their love story could have been described as a destructive type of fury.

Everyone has experienced fury on some level. Playing a competitive game, working, or being in a relationship – all take a type of fury. It's that feeling that you must try.

It's the force that gets you out of bed in the morning. Fury is the strive to be alive.

Chapter Five: A Lover's Insight

Insight is defined by Webster as,
"the power or act of seeing into a situation; penetration."

I DRAW INSPIRATION from others, the arts, and personal experience. As a sailor's family, we move around a lot and I need to be able to evoke inspiration in an instant. Moving is so aging. The average time at one location is three years; every three years we start all over again. I am currently on my sixth move.

Can you imagine starting over and over and over and over and over? To some, this is a dreamy thought. As long as I had my husband and son, I knew we were going to be ok in the end, but wow! I feel like I've experienced this life five times over.

One move, I was out-of-my-skin crazed and cranky from traveling all day when we finally reached our new home. The previous tenants were still there, moving out of the property. OMGosh ~ I went batty!

Taking some advice that was given to me as a teenager, I chose to breathe and let my husband handle the situation. I stayed in the car and just relaxed to music. What works for me may or may not help others under high pressure situations, but if you find the inspiration that works for you, practice it.

Experience is knowledge. We have met people of all genres and cultures. I am over-qualified in most positions I apply for. The job market for military spouses could not be more challenging. My advice is to keep your resume sparklingly simple. Don't mention or offer up too much information that isn't related to the job at hand. Only answer questions that are legally required at interviews, stay informed. For example, I've been asked, "Do you think being a mom will affect your abilities on the job?" We all know in real life the answer is, "Yes!" Children get sick, they get hurt, life happens, BUT prospective employers aren't allowed to ask that question.

So, my response was and still is, "At this time that is a non-issue."

A safe, polite way of saying, that is none of your business.

The struggle for women in today's job market is real. For sailor's wives, it can be downright cruel. Employers look at the timeline of your past jobs and can't understand it. I would watch their faces as I tried to explain, "As a spouse of an active duty military member, we move every three years. That's the reason that five different states are notated."

I cannot tell if it's a sense of wonder I see on their faces afterwards, a "not interested" expression because they knew I would be moving on in three years.

My late mother and her mother experienced much different challenges. During that time, ladies were more the caregivers and socialites. Women during this time were also gaining momentum for women rights and equality.

Today, this fight continues not only for women but for human rights.

One gains so much insight by experiencing something new. When you move, the learning is infinite.

As the saying goes, "When in Rome, do as the Romans do." Insight is gained if we have our minds open to it.

Every night I say the same prayer. It goes something like this:

"Dear Jesus,

I thank you for this day and all the things that you have made. I am grateful for all I have and every minute of every day. Please, Lord Jesus, continue to make me, shape me, and mold me to the person you desire me to be.

Amen"

As I pray this, I add any other problems we may be dealing with as well.

Sometimes my heart is so heavy, burdened by the negativity this world throws at us, but I try to always be open to change. Change is the only constant in our lives.

Don't wear this! Don't say that! Don't do that! Way too much to keep up with.

In moments like these, I remind myself to be the queen I am, straighten that tiara, and keep moving forward as myself! Taking my own advice. I have never stepped away from a challenge that I could foresee a gallant ending to. We've all been faced with these types of challenges. Whether it is at work or just trying to figure out what's for dinner. A sailor's wife faces all the same problems everyone experiences with determination and faith.

This, my friends, is where we find insight. A lover's insight must echo from within.

Trusting your intuition is of ultimate importance.

Once you start listening from within, your heart should feel like it's smiling and you start hugging people and moments with your eyes. The findings from within will bring you closer to your true self. Goals and dreams start to become a reality.

This sounds close to living in the land of unicorns, farting magic glitter powder everywhere that makes everything perfect. You can feel this, but you have to listen for it.

Insight.

Insight is taking your experience and goals all the while listening to yourself for you. Start by taking a situation that you have doubts about and someone wants you to do what they want but your insides are giving you warning signs, what should you do. Insight. You can agree with the other person and suffer the consequences, or you can listen to your gut and sleep well afterwards. Make hard decisions when needed and do what is best for you. Life is filled with these moments.

I want us all to succeed.

There are not enough of us out there with this mindset. If you are the Negative Nancy in your group, please repeat this statement:

"We all have good in us, we all have our own talents, as much as we are different, we all are truly the same."

Insight is keeping the bigger picture when the world only wants us to see what's on the news that night. There has been rape, murder, war, genocide, and so much more going on in our world since the beginning of time. TV and social media make it easy to view all this bad news.

It truly shapes our thoughts and lives. Please take this power back, please stop giving that part of you to the world that's not doing anything for you. It's a tough place to get out of when you realize you are being brainwashed. What you put into your mind can never be returned, replaced, or forgotten.

I understand that other aspects of our lives can have this same affect.

Our families, work, and anything we choose to put energy into can sometime be negative and normally at some point is.

I have been told from coworkers that I'm a horrible judge of character. These coworkers were the ones I should have watched out for. Those are warning words. I've also been told that I run circles around people and make my job look easy. These coworkers are the ones who usually want to be like you. I am all about paying forward anything I can. I want my friends and family to bring me treats to whatever retirement village that I end up in.

I recalling the time I found the perfect underwear.

You know what I'm talking about: the panty that feels good to wear and holds everything in the perfect way. I bought them all! I went home and ordered a set for every girl I knew. They thought I was just having an episode until they put them on.

Normally, if you find a treasure you keep it to yourself.

That's NOT what this series is about. Sharing is caring. Making moments count! Not the money spent but sharing something you found truly awesome. I was trusting my insight and being thoughtful, trusting my gut that my closest friends would love them, and they did!

Chapter Six: A Lover's Torment

Torment is defined by Webster as the "extreme pain or anguish of body or mind."

TORMENT CAN BE FUN, but it can also be painful; emotionally and physically. Mental health is just as important as physical health. Torment can strike in the form of stress, which is the number the one killer we humans face. It has negative, rippling physical effects on our body. When you have pain or stress in your life, it directly affects your mind, and the health of your body follows suit. It's not intentional, it's there, it's life.

My older sister is my hero. She raised two beautiful children. This girl is a super woman to me because she is dealing with a disability and has fought hard her whole life to be "normal."

What a crock! What the hell is normal these days? What torment we put on ourselves to be normal.

My sister was a single, working mother with children to care for. Torment was seeing her exhausted every day and seeing her babies upset when she felt like she wasn't enough.

This torment is real. I urge everyone who reads these memoirs to please use your health benefits and find someone to vent to. When you find the right person to share with, it can make your world a better place.

Torment is such a raw word and emotion. It's like the saying, "it hurts so good." like a stinging sensation. Torment can be addicting, but sometimes it's "drama" that we allow into our lives. I am very unattracted to drama, but drama always finds its way to me.

I'm not big on materialistic things, but I am high maintenance in my need for attention. Paying great attention to detail and knowing it makes all the difference.

Everybody likes when you take the time to say, "Good morning."

Stopping and asking, "How are ya?" or just a friendly smile.

Those moments seem few and far between these days. It feels like torment when I walk into a room and the tension this thick enough to cut with a knife.

Geesh…nothing can be this serious. I refuse to go out of this world a Grinchy raisin. REFUSE!

That's torment. I choose to be the difference. I choose to be that person who treats others the way I want to be treated. Say good morning, how are you, smile- even when you don't want to. I am not saying be ON all the time. No one can do that; but try. When you put the best version of yourself into the universe, it revives you. These different levels of highs and lows one feels can also give you a glimpse into yourself. You will notice a difference within. Take care of yourself. Love yourself, use the $10 sea salt body wash if you love it. Take a nap when you can, listen to yourself.

When you are kind to yourself and give yourself the same time you give others, torment can start to be fun.

It's not drama ~ that torment can be recognized as a type of foreplay. The teasing of a partner or the anticipation of an embrace.

At 18, still very much a young person mentally, I tormented my husband unintentionally. We met at a restaurant where we both worked. We were college students, each of us living on our own, and doing our own thing.

He swears that he fell in love with me instantly. His version is that I walked up to him while working, bit him on the shoulder and he was love-struck. Now, this *does* sound like something I would do, but I cannot confirm or deny this incident took place. He thought I was cute, and I thought, *This guy is a hunk*. He was a very kind, cunning guy who liked to have a good time.

I was not at all ready to jump into anything serious.

I was way too young mentally to recognize or reciprocate the love he felt. We became best friends and grew up together. He watched me make mistake after mistake and move from one relationship to another.

The love he had for me then was tormenting him, but he never gave up on me.

I remember telling him, "You never know what tomorrow will bring." I was just not ready, and I knew it.

Eventually, a dear friend sat me down and firmly said, "You must cut him loose if you aren't interested in him."

Basically, stop toying with this great guy's life and feelings. That night I thought about it and I couldn't imagine my world without him. By 23, we were married, bought a house, and were working our butts off to live the best life possible. He battled for me and now we both fight for us. I am so grateful to my dearly loved friend for talking some sense into me that night. I'm so happy that I listened to her and my heart. Trusting yourself can be hard. It takes practice.

My mother's story rang similar. In the '60s she met her high school sweetheart. She quickly was married and with child. Before the age of 20, she'd started her family.

Alone a lot due to my father's deployments, the torment presented its ugly side. She re-dedicated herself to her religion and was a beacon of light to many during tough times. My sailor father would come into port and also had needs…none of which were approved by the church. She kept an unaccompanied life when he was away, but wanted nothing more than to love him and his condition when he returned. She loved him enough for both of them, but he was a complicated person to love.

He did what sailors do best. Provided for the family, all the while protecting his country. This is heroic material. He also liked the partying part that came with being away so long – maybe what he had grown accustomed to. My father had an elevated testosterone rebellious kind of drive. This is when he became difficult.

I, personally, run from difficult situations and people, to this day because of him. I do not want anything to do with difficult people. This is my trigger word: "difficult!"

My father could have come home to his family rather than partying. He could have shown love to mother instead of this see-saw relationship he showed her.

Torment!

Chapter Seven: A Lover's Promise

Promise is defined by Webster as, "a legally binding declaration that gives the person to whom it is made a right to expect or to claim the performance or forbearance of a specified act."

IT TRULY HAD to be their marriage vows that kept them together. They shared their vows before God and their family. Faith helped my mother make it to the, "Until the death do us part" portion of their contract. Her promise to him was for forever.

Think about that word: promise. Promises are not supposed to be broken. A promise is an extra layer of commitment to whatever is at hand. I promised my child to protect and care for him forever. My husband expects me to honor my promise to him, and vice versa. Our promise is to love one another as we love ourselves. A lover's promise includes but isn't limited to, honoring each other's wishes. I want to treat my sailor like the king that he is in my world, but he knows that I'm also the person who can burn it all down.

Promises are imperative in a lover's world. Also, it's crucial that those promises are kept. If you cannot keep a promise, own it and let the people involved know. You will lose the relationship temporarily – maybe even permanently – but if you are forced to promise something you cannot commit to, you are getting yourself into trouble and setting yourself up for failure. Let's set ourselves up for success. Let's keep our promises. If it's too hard to do that; communicate it.

IT IS NOT WHAT YOU SAY, IT IS HOW YOU SAY IT! If you apologize with a sassy tone, it means nothing! If you do it in a dull tone, just to do it, it means nothing! If you say you're sorry, sincerely, you are forgiven. You know what your personal limits are; trust them. No one will take care of you but you, but you must listen and trust yourself. You matter.

A promise is also known as an assurance, an oath, or it can represent a type of security.

My mother's love for her children was compromised. I'm sure many children have had a great parent and then a not-so-great one. Sometimes rotating. Even though my father was a difficult man, my mother had the ability to keep all of her promises. I would hate when she kept secrets from me, but if she gave her word to someone, it was solid.

A person's word is all they have. If you break your word, most people wouldn't trust you again. It's simple. The only reason I would want to find out about what my mother promised to keep secret was because most times it left her physically and mentally upset. Stress kills, so I would try and help. I never liked or wanted to see my mother upset. It saddens me to think of all the times I may have caused this.

I am my mother when it comes personality traits. My personality falls mostly into the Extraversion/Intuition category. This group is described as:

"A responsible person who cares about others and is genuinely empathetic. You'd be a good teacher or philanthropist. You see the good in others and can sense when people are hurt or shy. You also exhibit leadership qualities and don't mind being the center of a room. You diagnose problems quickly and do your best to find solutions. You're also a planner and you like to stay current."

My mom was more than that and could steal the show by singing or playing the piano. She drew strength from her faith and was so creative. One can only aspire. She loved music and her TV shows. Near the end of her adventures upon Earth, she focused on her own spirit and mental health. Trying to finally get a fresh breath of air that was well-deserved, and one that she didn't have to work for.

She wanted for nothing, she needed nothing. The wants she did have were only to help others more. There is no bigger promise than that.

So selfless. So strong.

We all have this person in our realm of friends and family. We are pieces of carbon that attract others that are most like us. Sometimes this person isn't family nor a friend. Sometimes the person is the person we want to be. Imitate the qualities you most like in others. It's a great honor to replicate tidbits of ourselves to help others grow. I make this promise to you and my loving mother, "I promise to continue to share pieces of myself and help the next generation by loving unconditionally."

She did that for us and now we need to do it within our lives, too. My mom promised to always be here for me, and she was taken way too young. She was ready spiritually and mentally for the moment she left us.

She wasn't able to handle the physical world due to her ailments, but she promised to always be here, and now she is.

Chapter Eight: A Lover's Delight

Delight is defined by Webster as, "a high degree of gratification or pleasure."

IT'S MY BIRTH MONTH, and every birthday I seem to self-reflect all month about life. Doing a self-check mentally, spiritually, and physically for myself. There can be a lot of ups and downs while reflecting. That's why for my birthday I make myself go to the doctor get my annual physical. As uncomfortable as it is, it must be done yearly. I owe it to myself and the people I love to stay healthy. I demonstrate to my family how to take care of themselves by the way I take care of myself. The results give me a sense of peace. It makes me feel like I'm setting myself up for success for the year ahead.

When you have a physical, it is uber-important to be honest with your physician. The only person who knows your inside pain is you.

Please share these concerns and findings about yourself with a doctor of your choice. As we age (twenties, thirties, forties, fifties and so on), we grow and change. We morph into who we are supposed to be. We should be delighted to have another breath to breathe when so many cannot, and by choice, do not.

This birthday was especially hard-hitting, being the first birthday I didn't hear from my mother. No matter what she was dealing with or the problems she may have had, on this day or any of her children's birthdays, she would be there. She would either call or be physically with us; she always loved to acknowledge our day. Technically, she did all the hard work of carrying us to production, and then she loved us.

I had a dream last night and in this dream it was still my birthday and I noticed my mom hadn't called. *Wonder why my mom still hasn't called. I will call her.*

I always called my mother on my birthday to say "happy birthday" to her.

My heart sunk, as the awareness that mom was no longer present returned. However, I felt that it was her way of wishing me well from heaven.

I hope my mother knew the love our family had for her.

I look like my mother, and am delighted every time someone reminds me that I do. I'm proud to be part of my mom and part of my dad. I am very much like my father, but I look like my mother. My sailor father was not a delightful husband. He would regularly miss birthdays and holidays. Before I was born, he did take my mom to see her favorite music group, and a concert. They also tried to work on their relationship at a marriage retreat, but that was in extent of their quality time together. There were never any impromptu trips or dinners, nor were there any family vacations while we were children.

Once my siblings and I were old enough, we would make mom's birthday special.

Like all children, we tried to make her breakfast in bed, handmade gifts and cards with special heart-filled messages when we couldn't buy something. Those were her favorites. She loved to write, and she also had a lot to say. Here is a snippet from my mother that we can all implement, "Do your words match your actions?"

I can honestly say that I try my best to follow through and make the effort to match my actions with my words. That effort sets your intentions and sets your life pace.

I am so grateful and delighted to spend this birthday with my family. They treated me like royalty. The whole nine yards, breakfast in bed, gifts, parties, and the night ended with fireworks, actual fireworks. I relate my birthday with mother earth, as my birthdate falls on the first day of Fall.

The Autumnal Equinox means that this day, and only this day, has the same amount of daylight as night. I feel delighted in the Fall and love my birthdate and what it signifies.

My mother deserved her birthdays to be like this. When I saw the fireworks, I took them as a sign that this would be my best year yet. I love fireworks, and though I know my neighbors weren't thinking specifically of me when they set them off, I claimed the celebration for myself. I felt like my mother was also trying to wish me a happy birthday, too. It was delightful. I felt a weight lift while watching those bright fireworks.

Chapter Nine: A Lover's Lust

Lust is defined by Webster as, "an intense longing, usually intense or unbridled sexual desire."

EVERYONE FEELS LUST. Unbridled sexual desire sounds amazing to most women and men. Men and women sexually peak at different times, but sexual desire is natural. Whether fluid, bi, hetero or homosexual, desire is normal. Lust is a recognizable sensation and it can be addicting. Lust can be physically pleased as well as spiritually. Lust can also lead to problems, especially if it's one-sided. One-sided lust can lead to dangerous encounters like stalking or awkward run-ins.

Growing up as a naive girl, my presence and body language made men lust for me. As a teenager, I was approached in a mall to pose nude for a magazine. I declined, but even at that moment, no matter the amount of money offered, I knew that was not the route my life was going to take.

I had no money and could have easily accepted to better my home life, but at what cost?

In high school every boy thought they were in love with me. To say the least this made the girls despise me. It wasn't my fault, but it didn't matter. Size zero waist, blonde hair, green eyes, 5'0", and big boobs; I was just hating material. Now, I have a hate club that has monogrammed bedazzled jackets for new members. I mean, I literally did my laundry by water hose. No one knew that. There was a hole in the front door of our home from my father punching his way in. No one knew. I wore holey jeans and hand me down t-shirts every day to school, but it didn't stop lust. I took two suitors in high school, but I had many admirers. Two of them ended up moving schools because I wouldn't return their feelings. They could not understand that I had one boyfriend as a freshman and one boyfriend until I graduated. They felt like they had a right to me.

That is the bad lust, the dangerous lust.

I had no idea what I looked like or the impact I made or could make until after graduation. College and post-graduation life taught me a lot. I had guys after graduation come by my house and pitch their love to me. I turned all of them down. I guess you could say I was being selective. As women, this is one of our best qualities and men want it. They lust for it. The hard-to-get chick. Something that's easy to get isn't always the most valued.

We kept mom on her toes growing up. Imagine how hard it would've been to keep up with four offspring and their suitors. My sisters and I are very close in age. I am an Irish Twin, the middle girl, the one who took care of herself growing up. I'm the helper, the one who can make things happen, and the one who takes the lead, when needed.

Having four children, one must assume there was lust in our parents' relationship.

My sailor husband flew my parents and our family to his homeland in Nassau, Bahamas. This was my parents' first trip together since I was born and my mother's first time leaving the U.S. I was so happy to be able to share that time with them both. Please cherish your parents, how you treat them will ultimately be the way you will be treated when you grow older. Make the time to visit and chat with them often. You will never regret it. You will never regret making the effort to share your time with your parents. That trip had a happy tone and I lust for more of that.

I wish that type of lust for us all. I want us all to win. I want us all to feel love. Love can be messy. One lover is not another. Everyone has needs, desires, and want their feelings reciprocated. The same year we took my parents to the Bahamas, we visited Pennsylvania for a family reunion. My mother wanted to go, so, we made it happen.

That trip my father taught us about "deer grass" and had us all looking for it as we settled into the excursion.

We sang, and laughed most of that trip. Those were good times; my mother was happy there with her family that she hadn't seen in a very long time. Some since she was a little girl. She was just so content to be there, to be present amongst her people. Those moments revitalize you. When you can see someone's spirit lifting.

They remind us about where we came from, how far we've come, and confirm that we are indeed living in the moment. Spend time with your parents. You will never regret it. Do not put yourself into a harmful situation, but if you just try and do your best that's all one can ask of themselves.

A bittersweet moment just experienced, was a dream with my dearly, departed mother. We were standing in our kitchen here in New England, between the sink and the island.

She reached over to me and sweetly swept my face and said, "I am going to miss this smile."

I woke up instantly and cherished the thought of my mom doing that to me.

You see, my mom was the type of mom who would sing your praises to everyone else, but not to you. I knew that moment had never happened, but still what a sweet moment to have with her, even if it was just a dream. I've experienced many dreams where my mother would visit me. Sometimes I wake up sobbing and others I just wake up shell-shocked. This mourning period can last forever and feels like it fades in intensity day by day. However, the dreams of my subconscious affect my whole day.

Sleep is imperative for our health. I lust for a good night sleep. Could you imagine having a stress-free good night sleep every night? Maybe that's when we die? Maybe that's heaven?

This evening my sailor and I were enjoying this last-minute warming trend here in the Northeast. I looked toward the beach and saw neighbors enjoying their evenings walking the boardwalk. I remember walking that boardwalk with my mom every night. It was the perfect time for her. Her sweet hour.

The lighting has shifted outside to Fall. Darker earlier. The streetlights are all that keeps us seeing the boardwalk and street. We watched, together, the 2017 Autumn full moon rise over the Atlantic. The moon came up in an orange hue. By the time it was fully risen, the ocean was orange, like fire. It was a special moment and I will treasure it.

Chapter Ten: A Lover's Reality

Reality is defined by Webster as, "the world or the state of things as they actually exist, as opposed to an idealistic or notional idea of them."

RECEIVED OUR FIRST holiday magazine today. With sparkling pictures and so many things my mother would have loved.

This moment opened up the shock and awe of what happened last year. There are no words better than the ones spoken by my only brother at my sweet mother's service:

* * *

"I still don't believe it and I was there when it happened. As I've spent the past few weeks planning this celebration. Pouring over pictures, selecting music, creating this flower and candle garden up here.

My left brain knows very well that my heartbreak and sorrow will slip almost unnoticed into the vast pool of human experience, yet it is mine. She was my mother. Not someone else's – mine. It's a different day now. I could stand up here for hours and tell you about how I feel but that isn't what this is about… necessarily.

One of my favorite teachers, Richard Rohr, implores us to let life come at us. Stop resisting and make room for everything – because it all belongs. So, I try. I'm here today to experience and hold life – as it comes.

Life came in a big way on December 9th, 2017.

The day started with my personal joy at the sight of snow falling, and it was going to snow all day. I was thrilled.

We gathered as a family to go visit mom. She wanted a turkey sub with tomatoes. We stopped on our way to the rehab center to pick up the sub and a few other things.

When we arrived, the folks in the nurse stations saw me and said, 'Well, he's arrived!'

Apparently, mom had been talking about my visit and there is just a little family resemblance. I think they could have picked me out of a crowd as her son.

We all had a nice visit and I stayed behind. I had flown up to Boston and had just a handful of days to be there, so the plan was to spend the evening with her.

We went on a walk around the facility as part of her continuing physical therapy. We sat and talked by their huge Christmas tree in their common room and we talked about what they were serving for dinner that evening.

Crab cakes…and we talked about sharing them.

Snow continued to fall outside as dusk came and as snow does at dusk, turned everything a beautiful blue.

I had brought my wireless speaker to play Christmas carols and while they began to play, I turned to pick out which of the three windows in her room deserved the Christmas decorations I had brought with me all the way from Miami. While fiddling with a little Christmas tree, I chatted with her about my legendary Christmas decorating skills, how it wouldn't be right for Mr. Christmas to come visit and not decorate her room.

I turned around and she was gone.

My mother's last minutes were of blue snow falling, Christmas carols, and her son hanging decorations in her window.

All in all… not a bad way to go.

She was there for my first breath, and I was there for her last.

And this my friends, if I've ever seen it or experienced it… this is beauty.

Today would have been my parent's 48th wedding anniversary. It is partly why we chose this date. Dad passed on April 17, 2014, and we were all together to honor him. Mom and dad married young, and by the time they were 27 and 26 respectively, they had four young children.

Can you imagine?!? I'm the first born. For those who care to do the math… I'm 46… but don't tell anyone.

And as I've said many times, when I was five years old, my parents gave me a sister every year for three years.

She was a very active and dutiful military wife. Dad was out to sea most of every year… or so it seemed to my young mind.

She had put up a big map of the world on the wall and would take pins and yarn to map out his naval journey, telling us about the places he had been. When his ship would come in, we would join what seemed like thousands of other families waiting in the shipyard for their husband or dad to disembark from the huge aircraft carrier.

My mother always made it easy for him to find us. We had a big sign that said, 'The 4 Bs!'

It was an extraordinary experience for a young kid.

Huge ships, gigantic crowds, homecoming, and then leaving again to do it all again.

Mom was a very devoted churchgoer, so therefore, so were we. Sunday Morning, Sunday Night, Wednesday Night, and Friday Night.

I remember many times in the winter, my sisters would fall asleep on the way to church and that was just one too many girls for the two of us to handle. We'd have to have someone help get us all into the church. It was usually some young Navy man, like my father. Hauling three little girls who refused to wake up into the church.

My mom was a wonderful singer. I don't know if my sisters remember it well, but my mother was a part of a gospel trio that sang at different churches around the area.

I remember well the many hours of rehearsals in the empty church.

I vividly remember laying in the middle of the aisle, playing with the pattern in the orange and black carpeting while my mother and her trio sang and sang and sang.

This, of course, was the beginning of what became a vital part of my life; singing. In fact, my first solo was with that trio at the age of four years old.

A few years later, my mother taught me how to pick out harmonies by ear. I was thrilled! I got it! I heard it and I could sing it!

Just like those gospel singers who were always playing on my mom's 8-track cassette player. It was next-level stuff, people, and I knew it!

This is one of the best gifts my mother gave to me, and indeed singing changed the course of my life.

My mother picked the vast majority of music you have already heard and will hear in the rest of the service and at the reception.

She loved music... and I'm pretty sure it loved her back.

My mother was also very creative. She could put together eye-popping bulletin boards for our school and church. Displays that would leave you speechless. Anytime something needed decorated, my mother was one of the first calls.

This actually helped lead her to a long career with a grocery chain as pricing manager, in charge of retail displays, amongst other things.

One year, the ladies of the church got together, collected soup can lids and with a pair of crimpers, gold spray paint, and green and red yarn, they created the most amazing Christmas door decorations!

They sold like hotcakes and I can still remember the sound of those soup can lids, surprisingly musical.

Mr. Christmas came by his skills honestly and simply from my mother.

Now don't let me mislead you; it wasn't a bed of roses. Is it ever, for anyone? But those of you who know, know that the struggle was real, and the struggle was long.

There were very serious and chronic difficulties in her own childhood and in her marriage to my father.

As the song goes, *Go Rest High on that Mountain* says, 'I know in life, I know there was struggle.

And only you could know the pain. You weren't afraid to face the devil. You were no stranger to the rain.'

There were times of incomprehensible despair and suffering. It is not my intention to linger on the morbid, but I have a point in sharing this with you.

I think the most important thing I would want to know about my mother is that she was a survivor. Not a victim – no, that is a different thing altogether; she was a survivor. She had a deep well that in the most painful of times, she drew from."

"I could never put my finger on it, but I believe this was her love of God and her love for her family.

While some of her struggles may not have completely resolved in this life, my mother moved through her later years with a hidden dignity that I've only personally bumped into a few times.

When push came to shove, deep within her was a knowing, an absolute certainty of her divine heritage, and her worth. When I saw it, I was perplexed, I was amazed, but mostly, I was grateful. What a mystery this life is! So, life comes at us, indeed.

I want to share this little story. It was just a few months ago my mother told me a story from her childhood. My grandfather was also a Navy man, spending much of his time on submarines. When he was not at sea, there would be big picnics for the Navy families.

When my mother was very little, my grandparents would take her to these picnics, place her up on a picnic bench, and she would regale everyone with her marvelous little voice… singing…."

> 'You are my sunshine
> My only sunshine
> You make me happy
> When skies are grey
> You never know dear
> How much I love you
> Please don't take my sunshine away.'

I was so thrilled to hear this story of my mom singing as a little girl, and what I wouldn't give to hear her sing again.

These words are everlasting words and I know I was not alone in loving her."

* * *

My siblings and our families walked her ashes down the aisle to her shrine assembled from love to a song chosen by my mom.

The priest proceeded down the aisle and I followed closely behind carrying her urn.

I couldn't breathe. No moment in my life has been harder than that one. I was crying inconsolably. I truly did not think I would make it down the aisle way.

When I set her on the highest tiered table to be honored, a loud thump was heard through the church. The silence was deafening. I made it to my seat and just balled, I mean straight ugly cried.

The service continued with a magical candle lighting ceremony before anyone spoke. The candles around her and her relics were lit last. People from around the globe tuned into the live-streamed event. The piano played softly, played by a true lover of our family. The candles lit by a man who loves our family. The sweetest moment in such a hard, difficult day. Lit so methodically, the flowers all white and glorious.

The church dimmed, afternoon light shining through every stained-glass window. Dozens of white candles that took more than five minutes to lite around our angelic mother. Pianist slowed as the last candle was lit at her portrait. Loved ones still flowing in. It was silent and warm.

The priest started in the rear of the church, different.

No mic, so everything was so still. People continued to flow in. He quoted scriptures from the Book of Prayers. This was the priest who married my sailor and I. He proceeded down the aisle to his high chair. A friend read Psalm 31.

Silence.

A trio sung by dear friends with a starlet pianist accompanying them. Oh, this song ~ I felt like it was sung just for me. 'The Answer,' by Sara McLaughlin.

It was a breathtaking moment. I feel this song was chosen because everyone that knew my mother turned to her faith for guidance.

* * *

Tears flowing, my baby sister spoke first:

"Many may not know this, but my mother was one of my best friends. One of the hardest things I have had to adjust to is not speaking to her every day.

My mom has always been there for me and my family. I am deeply pained over losing her. It almost feels like I am running out of air at times. I can only hope and pray that one day I will share a relationship with my children like the one I shared with her. I will always cherish my mother's support and her love that she has shown to me and my family.

I am comforted in my heart that she is here with me today. I believe she and my father are here guiding me day by day as this life moves on.

I will always miss you. Life is sometimes unfair. It is my prayer that my family and friends realize that life is such a gift. I pray that you are always loved and you live your life to the fullest with as much joy and happiness as possible. I know in my heart that our loved ones who are in heaven now are with us.

Until we meet again, mom and dad."

* * *

My oldest sister followed with a touching reading from the Bible: II Corinthians 5:17, Revelation 21:4, II Timothy 4:7-8.

Then her, voice quivering, she said:

"When I was with my mother the days I was in the hospital with her before the procedure and after, we always prayed and worshipped God.

We always quoted Bible scriptures for encouragement, strength, and peace. That's who she was, a great example to us all by her faith. I have a message from my mom for everyone here.

'I am sorry that I left you. I know you feel alone. God told me that he needed me. He called me to come home.

And what seemed to be an instant, in a twinkling of an eye, an angel gently took my hand and led me toward the sky. As I ascended into heaven, beyond the pearly gates. The angels were rejoicing. Then I saw his radiant face. God's eyes shown down upon me from the glory of his throne.

He said, enter into paradise because heaven's now your home.

I fought the fight, I finished the race. Throughout the trial, I kept my faith. No longer do I suffer; my body's been made whole. I am flying with the angels and Heaven's now my home. God told me not to worry. He said, 'you'll be ok because eternity is forever, and we'll meet again someday.

I fought the fight, I finished the race. Throughout the trial, I kept my faith. No longer do I suffer; my body's been made whole. I am flying with the angels and heavens now my home.

I am flying with the angels and heavens now my home.'"

* * *

That was tough to follow. It was my turn and I had just a quote. A quote!

"My mother was residing with me when she passed away.

This has been a huge journey for me, but I found something that resonated.

'Grief. I have learned is really just love. It's all the love you want to give but cannot.

All that unspent love gathers up in the corner of your eyes, in the lump of your throat, and in the hallow part of your chest. Grief is love with no place to go."'

* * *

My musically-inclined brother sang a sweet ballad in honor of our confidante. He played the piano and sang so bittersweetly.

As the service continued, the lighting became more magical. A family friend read, *When Sorrow Comes*.

The priest also knew my mother. His reflections are always well respected. They were personal and passionate. The blue, red, and green lights poured upon him.

The candles were now well lit and bright. The white flowers were enchanting.

His personal words for her were special.

* * *

"And so, it was for a beautiful baby girl. Her father was in the Navy and her family transferred from place to place. In the process her family was exposed to many different ways of life that ordinary children knew nothing about.

This gave her, an extraordinary, sensitive child, a broader way of seeing the world around her. An appreciation of other people and how they lived that she never lost.

She met her inseparable companion, the son of a Pentecostal minister, and eventually they were married.

From this union, four beautiful lives emerged. Creative lives, spectacular ones, and soon she found herself single-handling managing this family of four children. Each with very different personalities, while her husband was out at sea.

Though there were rough times and sometimes very hard ones, they stayed together until her sailor's death. At that time, she moved in permanently with her daughter and spent the last years in Massachusetts, not too far away from the town where she was born.

Her life not only participated in creating four new lives but touched others with a wisdom, born out of the suffering that truly embracing and living life creates for each one of us.

Even when things were at a low point for her, she knew how to celebrate.

She continued to do so with a contagious verve that had a way of bringing many people out of their own little dark places of suffering and hurt. During her last years among us, she dedicated herself to personal growth and was constantly seeking new dimensions of life and truths, which she shared with her friends and family.

She didn't just sit around the fire and become a couch potato. She was working on herself to the very end and as a result new ideas, new thoughts grew from her efforts to grow to become more than she was.

It would be hard to meet a more loving and generous person than her. From the time I met her, she was constantly giving and sharing, not just a little bit, but all that she had with those close to her. I expect that generosity will continue toward all who she loves even though she has moved into a different dimension.

After her procedure, she quite suddenly and unexpectedly left this world, and now lives on in a new place. In a new and fuller spiritual reality. Her soul has made the transition from this world, with all of its mixed experience, to a land where all is light."

Paraphrasing Rumi:

...she has died to the den and noise of mundane concerns and now in the silence of love, she glows with the spark of divine light.

We are grateful for having known you. We are thankful your life has touched ours. We will cherish your memory and treasure the things your love has given us. As your journey continues into another realm, may you be blessed for all that you have left behind in this one. May your beautiful soul rest in the peaceful joy of the divine presence.

May you and I remember her through our own love and generosity that have grown and expanded because she was a part of our life's experience. Thank you, we will miss you and always keep you close to our hearts."

* * *

A duet of "The Prayer" closed the Father's message.

The music shared during mom's celebration was played live.

This final service was perfect for my mother. Her loved ones loved her, probably more than themselves. I see her smile and feel her love everywhere. That is what losing a major link in your family will do. You see them everywhere, every day. I hope she does walk amongst us. We need her in our lives. We miss her dearly.

The last responsive reading was from Jewish liturgy, *We Remember Them*, read by an adored family member.

This is the best way to imagine what it means to see or feel your loved ones after they are gone. The words remind us to honor those whom we love that are no longer with us. Remembering as we live and love our loved ones soul live on in and through us.

* * *

"In the rising of the sun, and in its going down, we remember them. From the moment I wake till I fall asleep, all that I do is remember them.

In the blowing of the wind and in the chill of winter, we remember them. On the frigid days of winter and the moments I breathe the cold air, I warm myself with their embrace, and remember them.

In the opening of buds and in the rebirth of spring, we remember them. As the days grow longer and the outside becomes warmer, I am more awake and I remember them.

In the blueness of the sky and in the warmth of summer, we remember them. When I look above and see the images of the clouds and when I am comforted by the sun that shines down on me, I remember them.

In the rustling of the leaves and in the beauty of autumn, we remember them. From the time in which I feel the cool, crisp breeze and see the colors of the leaves, I remember them.

In the beginning of the year and when it ends, we remember them. On the day I make resolutions for myself and on the day I reflect upon how I've grown, I remember them.

When we are weary and in need of strength, we remember them. As I am faced with challenges that enter my life, I remember all that they taught me, and remember them.

When we are lost and sick at heart, we remember them. When I have gone astray and feel uncomfortable, I ask for help and remember them.

When we have joys we yearn to share, we remember them. From those times of celebration, love, and happiness, I remember them.

So long as they live, we, too, shall live, for they are now a part of us, as we remember them. On every day, and in every way, I know that they are with me and I remember them."

* * *

The priest said the closing prayer and the piano played my mother's favorite hymn, "It is well with my soul."

While the piano played, the candles were slowly snuffed out and friends and family began to leave. The last candle was left lit beside my mother and her portrait.

I stood, waiting in the back of the church to say goodbye to loved ones who journeyed to see her and be with us. The lighting was blue from the stained-glass windows. A slide show played of pictures of mom with her family and friends.

I waited until the last person leaves and then changed to catch the next flight back to Boston.

* * *

This feels like a dream, not real. Even now it's surreal. One holiday magazine and I turn to liquid. Words to live by, yesterday is in the past, today is a present, tomorrow is gift. Make each moment count.

Turn the page for a Sneak Peak of

A Sailor's Wife

Volume Two

Coming Valentine's Day, 2019

A Sailor's Wife

Volume Two

Written by: B.L. Fleischer

Chapter One: A Lover's Romance

Romance is defined by Webster as, "to court or woo; a quality or feeling of mystery, excitement, and remoteness from everyday life."

AS A CONFIDENT, gorgeous, young, and broken female who knew absolutely nothing, I had a feeling of loss in this world that has so much to offer. I knew at a very young age that I was not going to have the same problems that many before me had self-inflicted upon themselves. I have seen relationships implode before their first kiss. I was watching for clues and patterns of behavior that triggered a fight or an outcome that I did not want for myself.

I am a third-generation sailor's wife; my mother was married to a sailor, and her mother before me. Heaven is where we treasure them now. The ebb and flow of this lifestyle is tough.

In my late teenage years and early twenties, I met my husband of 20-plus years.

This man adored me. We were both college students, living on our own – separately, and working to make ends meet. He was experienced in mannerisms and properly raised. Born and raised in the Bahamas and a priest's son to boot. He is so good and pure. An exotic Bahamian hunk. Multi-cultured and unique, a true gentleman. At that time though, other men were flocking to me. I was not committed to anyone and could have had a different suitor every night if I had chosen.

There was a blue-blooded country bumpkin, a red-blooded American cop, a US Marine, a crooked Italian chef, a Jewish millionaire, a brooding Irishman in construction, a partying Puerto Rican, a possessive Salvadoran, and a Bahamian hunk who had most of my attention.

All so vastly different, including their romantic ways.

A special thank you to my BETA team!

N. Bokun

B. Bonello

T.C. Fleischer

Z.C. Fleischer

R.J. Holcombe

W. Garfinkle

W.P. Mitchum

L.A. Parker

C.M. Reese

C. Sykes

www.ingramcontent.com/pod-product-compliance
Lightning Source LLC
Chambersburg PA
CBHW052027290426
44112CB00014B/2407